GEOGRAPHYWISE

RIVERS

Leon Gray

WAYLAND

First published in 2010 by Wayland

Wayland
Hachette Children's Books
338 Euston Road
London NW1 3BH

Wayland Australia
Level 17/207 Kent Street
Sydney, NSW 2000

Series Editor: Rasha Elsaeed
Designer: Tim Mayer, MayerMedia
Illustrator: Peter Bull Art Studio
Consultant: Meg Gillett

British Library Cataloguing in Publication Data

Gray, Leon.
Geographywise.
Rivers.
1. Rivers--Juvenile literature.
I. Title
910'.021693-dc22

ISBN 9780750262644

Printed in China

Wayland is a division of Hachette Children's Books, an Hachette UK company.

Picture acknowledgements
p1 01095642 (repeat p6) © Xi Zhi Nong/naturepl.com, p4 (tr,b) © ISTOCK, p5 (tl,tr,br,bl) © ISTOCK, p6 01095642 (repeat p1) & back cover © Xi Zhi Nong/naturepl.com, p7 (t) © NASA, p7 (b) © ISTOCK, p8 © ISTOCK, p9 © Wayland Diagram, p10(l,br) © ISTOCK, p11 © ISTOCK, p11 (l) © Wayland Diagram, p12 (t) © Wayand Diagram, p12 (b) © ISTOCK, p13 © Wayland Diagram, p14 © 10175337 Astromujoff/Getty Images, p15(t) © 01236097 Merryn Thomas/ Bluegreenpictures.com, p15 (b) © 01236104 Merryn Thomas/ Bluegreenpictures.com, p16(t) © ISTOCK, p17(t, b) © ISTOCK, p18 © 01207495 BenoitStichelbaut/ Bluegreenpictures.com, p19b © 08110962 Roberto Rinaldi/Bluegreenpictures.com, p19(t)+ cover © 981545-001 David Frazier/Stone/Getty Images, p20 © ISTOCK, p21(t,b) © ISTOCK, p22 42-16971959 ©Xiaoyang Liu/Corbis , p23(t,b) © ISTOCK, p24 42-15733780 © Irwin Thompson/Dallas Morning News/ Corbis, p25 42-18078417 © Diego Azubel/epa/Corbis, p26 © 86046629 Anne Rippy/Getty Images, p27 DWF15-507554 © Amit Bhargava/Corbis

Disclaimer
The website addresses (URLs) included in this book were valid at the time of going to press. However, because of the nature of the Internet, it is possible that some addresses may have changed, or sites may have changed or closed down since publication. While the author and Publisher regret any inconvenience this may cause the readers, no responsibility for any such changes can be accepted by either the author or the Publisher.

Contents

What are rivers?

Rivers are bodies of fresh water that flow in channels, from a high point, such as a mountain or a hill, down to the sea. Most begin as tiny streams that trickle down slopes. Many become giant waterways that snake across the land.

Rivers are found all over the world. They are home to all sorts of wildlife. Many plants and trees grow by rivers and animals use the river for food and drink.

WORLD'S LONGEST RIVERS

This table shows the longest river in each continent.

River	Continent	Length
Nile	Africa	6,650 km (4,132 miles)
Amazon	South America	6,400 km (4,000 miles)
Chang Jiang (Yangtze)	Asia	6,300 km (3,915 miles)
Mississippi	North America	3,780 km (2,350 miles)
Volga	Europe	3,530 km (2,193 miles)
Murray	Australia	2,530 km (1,572 miles)

Source: http://www.britannica.com

Rivers are lifelines for people, too. They provide us with food, such as fish, and water to drink and to grow crops. Most settlements were built along rivers.

Throughout history, rivers have been important travel routes for transporting goods and people from place to place. A river's flowing water can also be used as an energy source to generate electricity.

From mountain to sea

The start of a river is called the source. This is usually a tiny, fast-flowing stream on high ground, such as a mountain. Some rivers begin where a natural **spring** releases water from under the ground. Other rivers start from a lake, where rain water and melting ice and snow collect and feed the stream.

As the water flows downhill, small streams join with larger ones and are called **tributaries**. A river grows as it collects water from its many tributaries.

When the river reaches lower ground, the land flattens out and the river gets wider.

A highland stream tumbles down the slopes of these mountains in Yunnan Province, China.

*This satellite image shows the Nile **Delta**, where the River Nile flows into the Mediterranean Sea.*

The water flows more slowly over the land, forming S-shaped curves, called **meanders**. The route a river takes is called its course.

Most rivers end when they flow into a large body of water, such as a lake or the sea. The end of a river is called its mouth.

UNBELIEVABLE!

Some of the Earth's largest rivers drain into the Atlantic Ocean. They include the Amazon and the Mississippi. In fact, nearly 50 per cent of the Earth's river water drains into the Atlantic!

A river snakes over the land as it flows along its course.

The water cycle

Rivers are an important part of the water cycle. The water cycle is the journey water takes to circulate around as it constantly moves between the air, land and sea.

UNBELIEVABLE!

Only 1 per cent of the water on the Earth is fresh water that people can drink. Most of the water on our planet is in the seas and oceans, and is too salty to drink.

Some of the water that falls as ***precipitation*** *seeps through the ground, where it collects as an underground water store, called groundwater.*

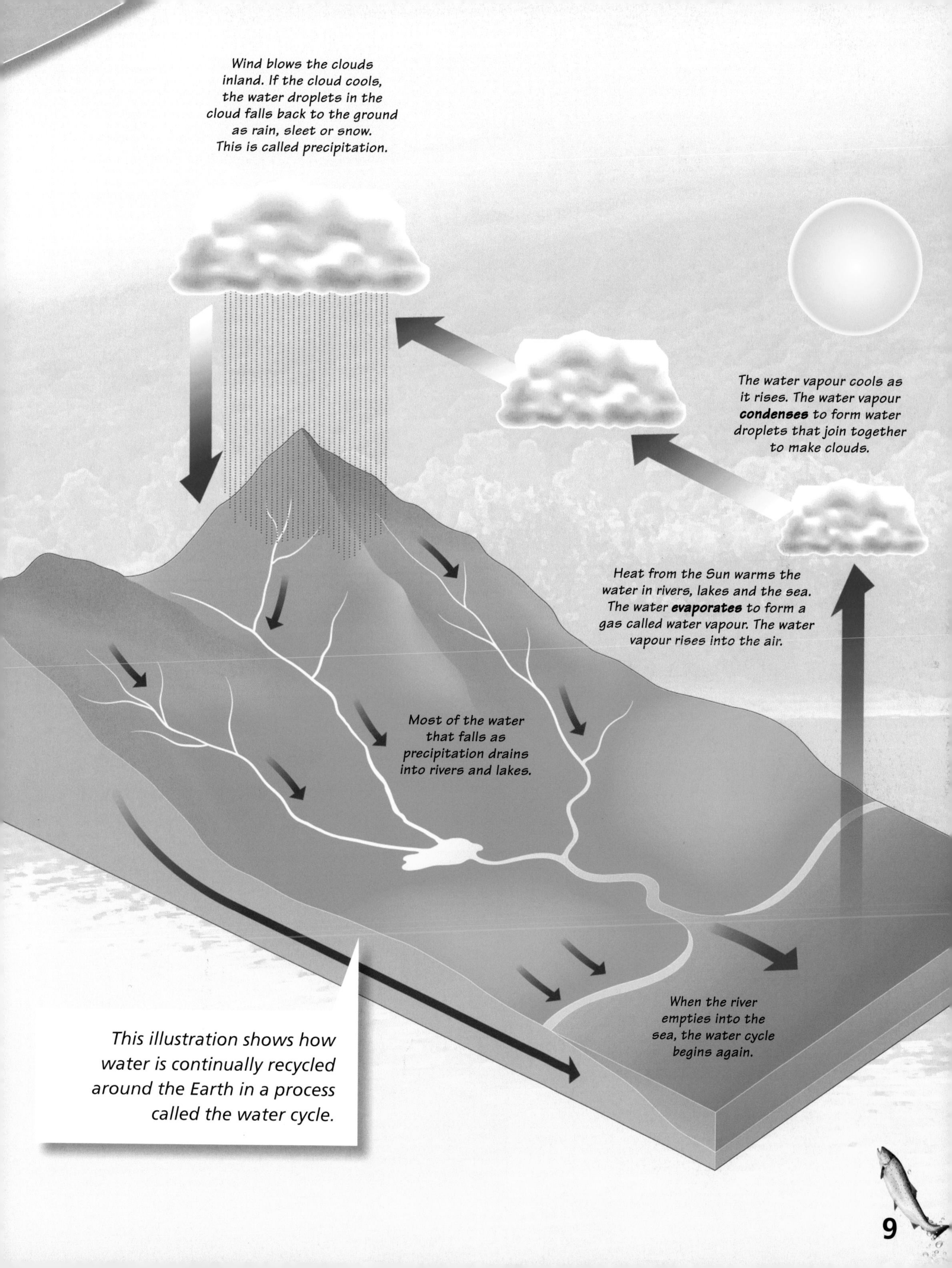

This illustration shows how water is continually recycled around the Earth in a process called the water cycle.

Shaping the land

Rivers shape the land in a process called **erosion**. When a river flows over the ground, the water picks up loose rocks, stones and gravel and erodes its channel. All the material in the water is called the **load**. The river carries the load along in the **current**. This process is called **transportation**.

As the river flows downstream, the load scrapes along the river bed. Over thousands of years, the river erodes deep, V-shaped valleys in the land.

The Charyn River carves a canyon through the barren landscape of southern Kazakhstan.

Rapids are shallow, fast-flowing sections of a river where rocks and boulders stick out of the water.

A **waterfall** forms when a river flows over hard rocks, then over soft rocks. The river erodes the soft rock and creates a cliff. As the water tumbles over the cliff, it erodes the rock at the bottom. This creates a deep pool called a **plunge pool**.

This illustration shows a cutaway through a waterfall. Water cascading over the waterfall carries sand and small pebbles that erode the soft rock at its base, forming a plunge pool.

Niagara Falls is a spectacular waterfall that straddles the border between Canada and the United States.

ON A TIGHTROPE...

Frenchman Jean-François Gravelet (1824–1897) was the first person to walk over the Niagara Falls on a tightrope. He made the crossing on 30 June 1859. He was known as the Great Blondin because of his shocking blond hair.

On the flood plain

As the river flows along its course, the slope of the land levels out. The water slows down, and the river starts to weave across the **flood plain**. The land around the river is called the flood plain because the river can spill over its banks and flood the land – particularly after heavy rainfall.

A river forms S-shaped meanders as it flows across the flood plain.

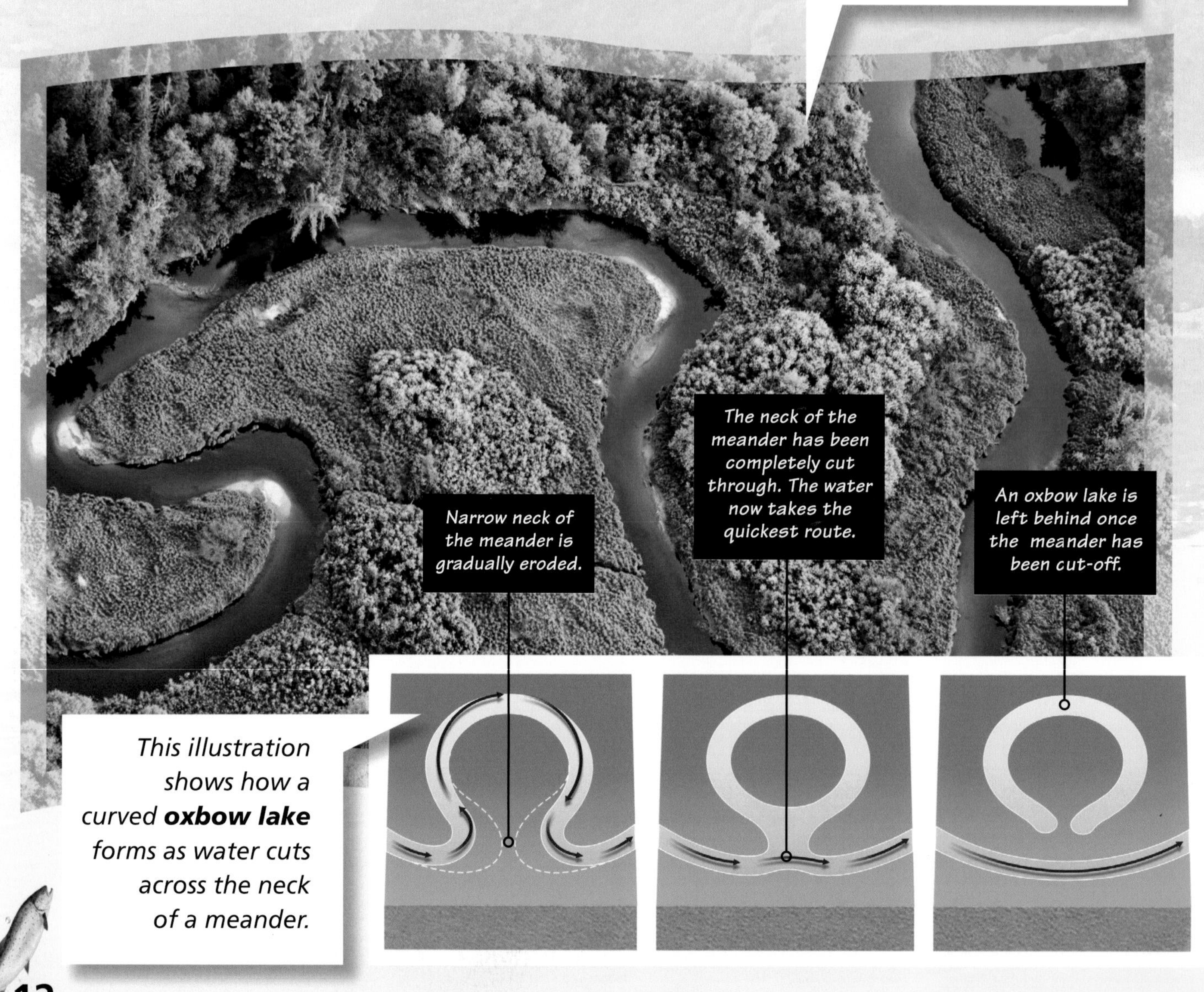

*This illustration shows how a curved **oxbow lake** forms as water cuts across the neck of a meander.*

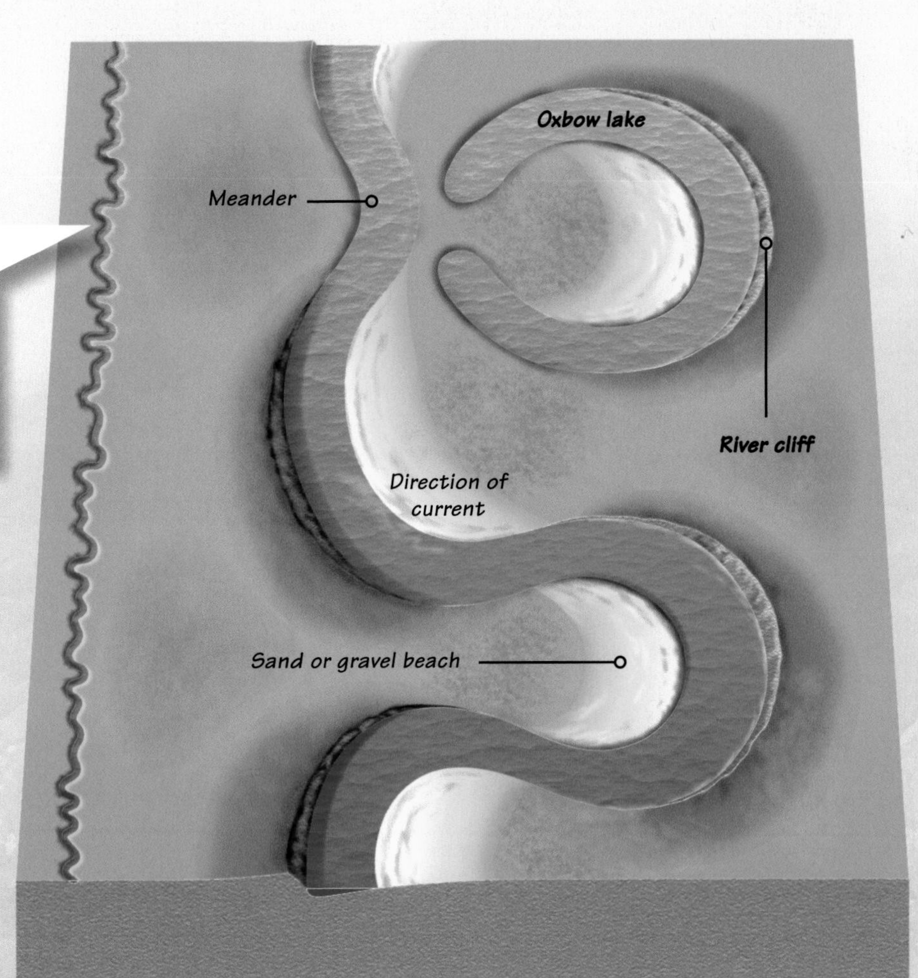

This illustration shows some of the features found on a flood plain.

A river flows across the flood plain in S-shaped bends called meanders. The water flows more slowly on the inside of the bend. The river **deposits** pebbles, sand and **silt** there to form a sand or gravel beach. The water moves more quickly on the outside of the bend. Here the current erodes the rock to form steep banks called **river cliffs**.

The river is able to change its course during and after heavy rain because its current is stronger at these times. When the river cuts straight across a meander it forms a curved oxbow lake.

UNBELIEVABLE!

Lake Chicot in Arkansas, USA, is the largest natural oxbow lake in North America. The lake is 32 kilometres (20 miles) long and 1.2 kilometres (three quarters of a mile) across. The lake formed hundreds of years ago as the Mississippi River cut across one of its meanders.

A river meets the sea

When a river meets the sea, the river mouth may widen into an **estuary**. This is where the river drains fresh water into the ocean. The **tides** wash salt water into the mouth of the river. This mixture of salt water and fresh water is called brackish water.

By the time the river meets the sea, the water is full of **sediment**. This is the sand, silt and clay that forms as pebbles and gravel break up in the water current. The river moves very slowly at it reaches the sea, and so the river dumps the sediment where it may build up to form a delta.

The River Nile dumps its sediment into the sea to form a triangular delta.

WHAT'S IN A NAME?

The Greek historian Herodotus (who lived in the 5th century BCE) gave deltas their name more than 2,500 years ago. He compared the shape of the mouth of the River Nile to the triangular letter delta (Δ) in the Greek alphabet.

A delta is a wide, flat area of sand or silt where the river splits up into many smaller channels. Most deltas are shaped like triangles, but there are more unusual shapes, such as the lobate delta (shaped like an earlobe) and the bird's foot delta (shaped like a bird's foot).

These photographs show the River Looe estuary in Cornwall at low tide (top) and high tide (bottom).

Low tide

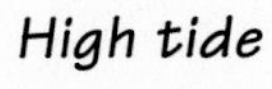

High tide

River wildlife

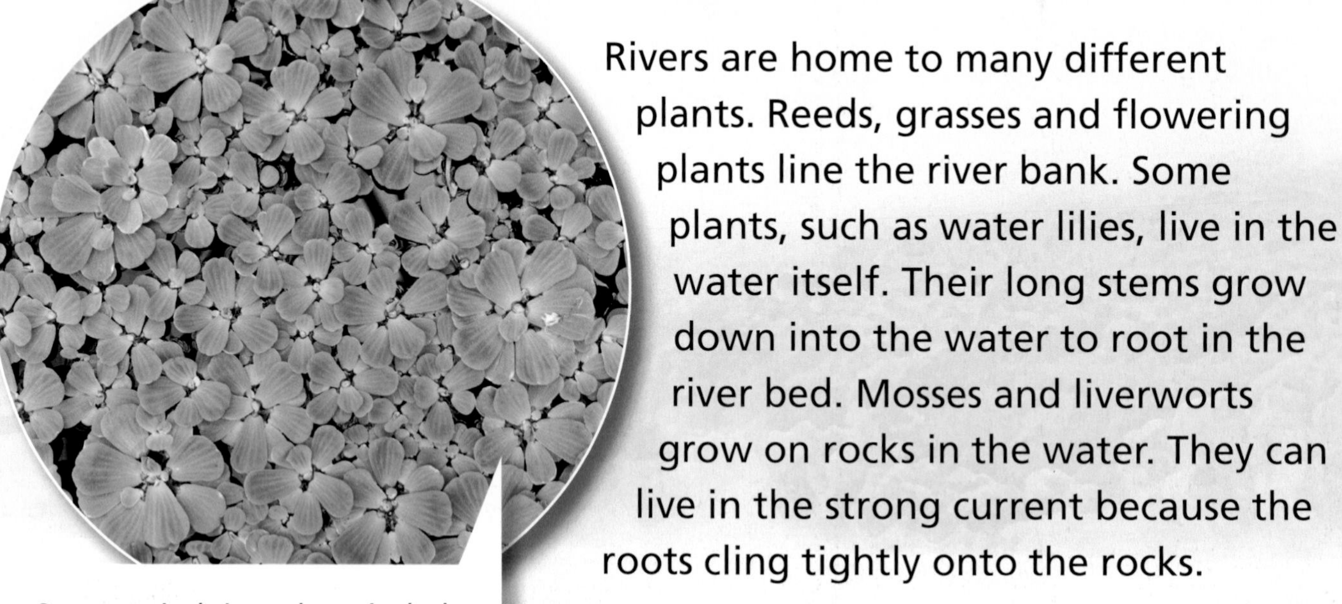

Rivers are home to many different plants. Reeds, grasses and flowering plants line the river bank. Some plants, such as water lilies, live in the water itself. Their long stems grow down into the water to root in the river bed. Mosses and liverworts grow on rocks in the water. They can live in the strong current because the roots cling tightly onto the rocks.

Some typical river plants include duckweed (above), reeds, river birch, and water lilies.

A heron wades through the shallow water of a river, stabbing at fish and frogs with its long, sharp bill.

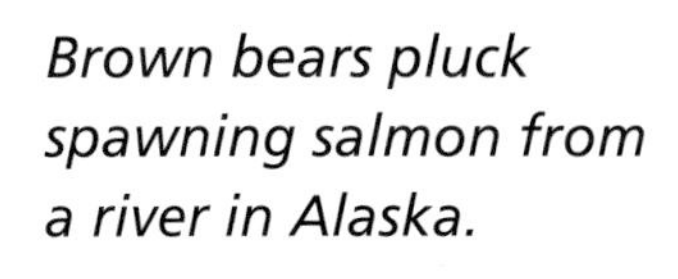

Brown bears pluck spawning salmon from a river in Alaska.

Many animals live in or near rivers. Fish live in the water all the time but frogs and many insects only spend part of their lives in the water, leaving when they become adults. Other animals visit the water to find food. Birds, such as herons and kingfishers, hunt fish from the river. Bears fish for salmon and mammals, such as otters and voles, live in burrows along the river bank.

In some countries, dangerous animals live in rivers. Alligators hunt in the rivers of Florida in the United States and parts of China. Hippopotami are aggressive animals that live in the rivers and lakes of southern Africa.

UNBELIEVABLE!

There are more species of fish in the Amazon River than in the entire Atlantic Ocean. The forests around the Amazon are also home to almost one-third of all the world's bird species.

The alligator is a dangerous predator that lives in rivers of the southeast USA.

Living by rivers

The bustling city of Brest in France is built on the banks of the River Penfeld.

Rivers are important to people. Many of the world's cities grew from small villages located along rivers. Villagers used the water to drink and to clean themselves and their clothes. People also fished the rivers for food and hunted animals that visited the river for drinking water.

Rivers are also important for farming. During a flood, a river deposits a thick layer of mud and silt on the flood plain. This makes the flood plain fertile. Rivers provide water for crops to grow. In the past, farmers dug narrow channels to bring the water to their fields. This is called **irrigation**. The ancient Egyptian civilization developed as a result of the yearly flooding of the River Nile.

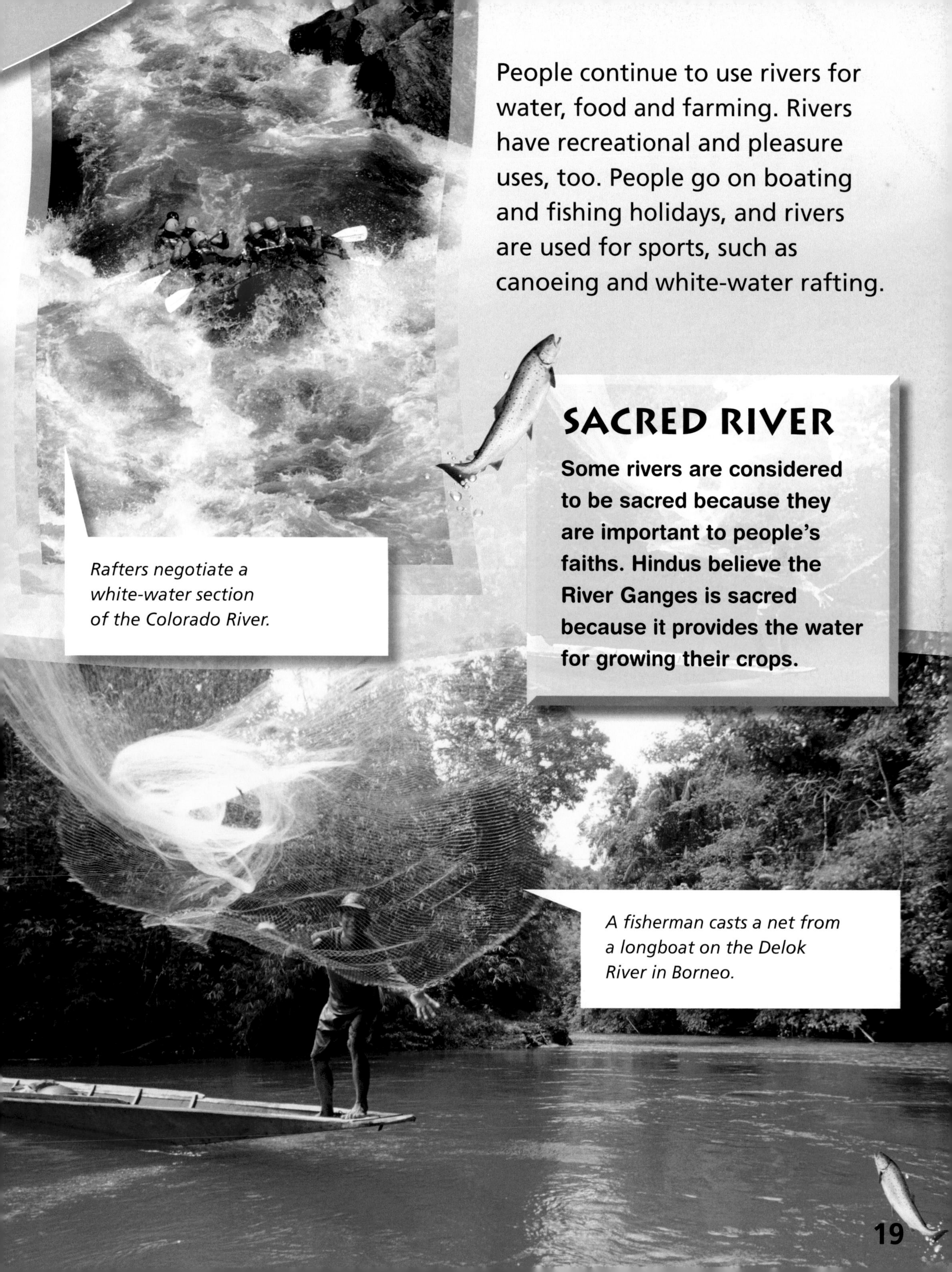

People continue to use rivers for water, food and farming. Rivers have recreational and pleasure uses, too. People go on boating and fishing holidays, and rivers are used for sports, such as canoeing and white-water rafting.

Rafters negotiate a white-water section of the Colorado River.

SACRED RIVER

Some rivers are considered to be sacred because they are important to people's faiths. Hindus believe the River Ganges is sacred because it provides the water for growing their crops.

A fisherman casts a net from a longboat on the Delok River in Borneo.

Moving around

Rivers were once the only way of getting around. Travelling by boat was much quicker and easier than walking across the land.

The earliest boats were probably floating logs tied together with reeds. Soon, people started to hollow out logs to make dugout canoes. Early explorers travelled by boat to places no one had ever been before. New villages appeared when people settled in these newly discovered places.

RIVER EXPLORERS

In 1804-06, American explorers Meriwether Lewis (1774–1809) and William Clark (1770–1838) travelled 3,725 kilometres (2,315 miles) up the Missouri River, over the Rocky Mountains and then down the Columbia River to the Pacific Ocean. They made maps of the land they had crossed.

The Staten Island Ferry transports New Yorkers between Staten Island and Manhattan.

Canal boats transport people around the water township of Bangkok, Thailand.

Today, people use rivers to carry goods such as crops, heavy machines and raw materials from place to place. Transporting goods on rivers is cheaper than using roads and railways.

Canals are man-made waterways which are also used to move goods and people from place to place. The Panama Canal connects the Atlantic Ocean in the east with the Pacific Ocean in the west. Using the canal saves a lot of time, because ships do not have to sail all the way round South America.

Thousands of vessels navigate the Panama Canal every year, transporting cargo around the world.

River power

People have used the power of rivers for hundreds of years. They built huge water wheels that turned as water flowed over them. This provided the power to grind grain into flour. Later, the power of moving water was used to drive machines to saw timber or weave cloth.

UNBELIEVABLE!

The world's biggest **dam** is the Three Gorges Dam on the Yangtze River in China. It is 2.3 kilometres (1.4 miles wide) and 185 metres (605 feet) tall. The reservoir behind the dam is more than 600 kilometres (375 miles) long.

Water gushes through a section of the Three Gorges Dam in Hubei Province, China. Turbines in the power station convert the energy of the flowing water into electricity.

In the twentieth century, scientists discovered how to make electricity using flowing water. They built a dam across a river. When water flows through narrow channels in the dam, it turns huge **turbines**. As the turbines spin, they turn generators, which produce electricity.

The flowing water of the Colorado River drives the turbine blades of these generators at the Hoover Dam in the United States.

Electricity made by using the power of moving water is called **hydroelectricity**. The advantage of hydroelectric power (HEP) is that is does not cause **pollution**. The river water builds up behind the dam, forming a lake called a **reservoir**. This provides drinking water and a place for people to enjoy water sports, such as sailing. However, building dams can destroy natural **habitats** and floods valleys, forcing people to move from their homes.

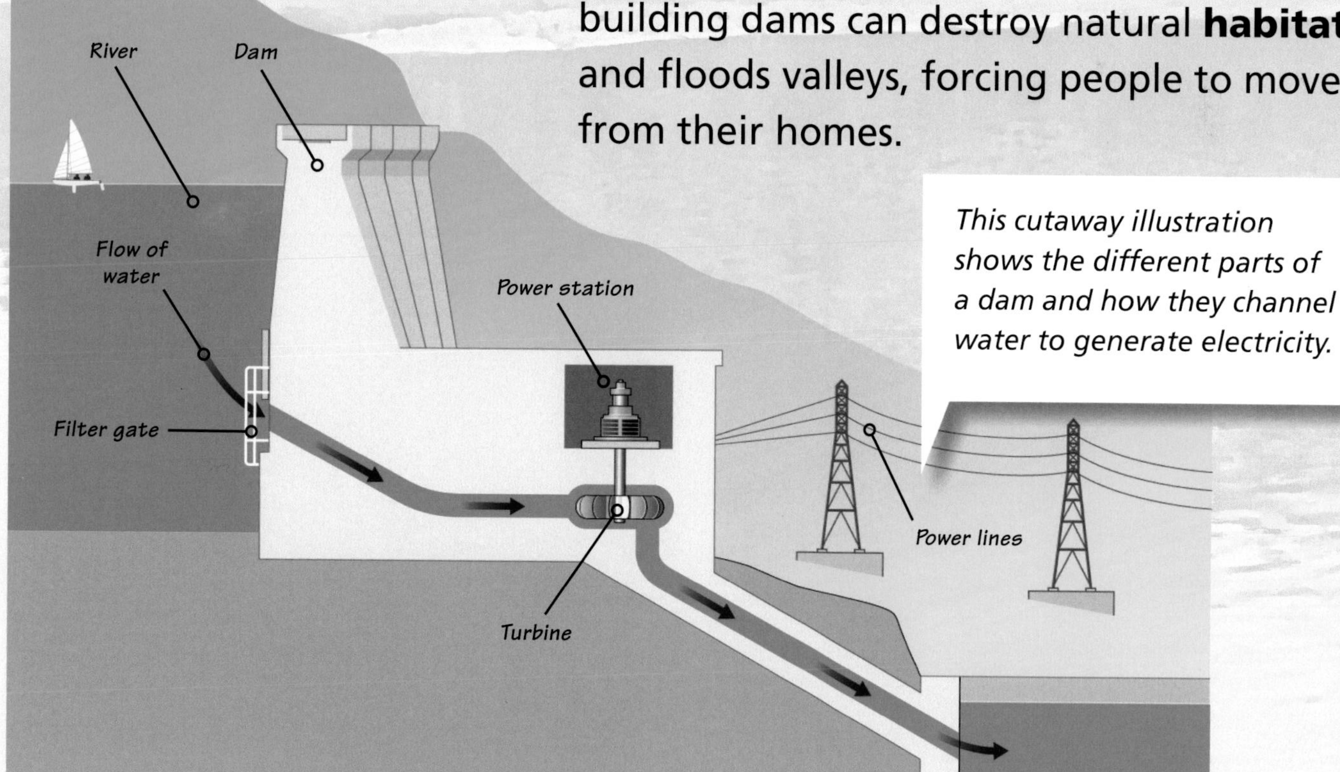

This cutaway illustration shows the different parts of a dam and how they channel water to generate electricity.

Problems with rivers

Floods are part of the natural cycle of all rivers, but they can cause problems for people who live on riverside locations. When a river floods, the force of the water and all the sediment in it can wash away everything in the river's path. A serious flood can knock over trees and damage homes and farmland.

Flash floods result from sudden heavy rainstorms and can kill people and destroy towns. The water rises so quickly that people do not have time to escape.

Heavy rains from Hurricane Katrina caused the River Mississippi to flood the city of New Orleans, Louisiana, in August 2005. More than 1,500 people were killed.

*People walk across the dried-up bed of the Jialing River in the city of Chongqing in China. The river dried up following a **drought** in 2007, which left millions of Chinese facing water shortages.*

Some scientists think that **global warming** is changing our weather. When people burn **fossil fuels** in cars, factories and homes, carbon dioxide and other gases are released into the air. These gases trap heat from the Sun, and scientists believe this is changing global weather patterns.

Some parts of the world are getting more rain, with floods and storms becoming more common. Other places are getting less rain and so rivers are drying up. When this happens over many years, it is called a drought.

THE MONSOON

Every year, heavy rains called monsoons provide more water than rivers can transport, causing severe flooding in Baglahesh and India.

Damaging rivers

Rivers provide some of our most beautiful natural habitats. They are important in supporting the survival of plants and animals, people and communities. Yet, many rivers are polluted by human activities, such as farming, industry and even tourism.

Factories and farms may leak poisonous chemicals into rivers. Waste water draining from homes is mixed with cleaning products, which makes the pollution worse.

SAVE WATER!

Reducing the amount of water your household pours down the drain will limit the amount of pollution you introduce to your local river.

- **Do not leave the tap on when you brush your teeth.**
- **Have a shower instead of a bath.**
- **Encourage your parents to fix leaking taps.**
- **Collect rainwater to water plants.**

The litter people drop into rivers, lakes and canals damages these habitats, affecting the plants and animals that live in the water.

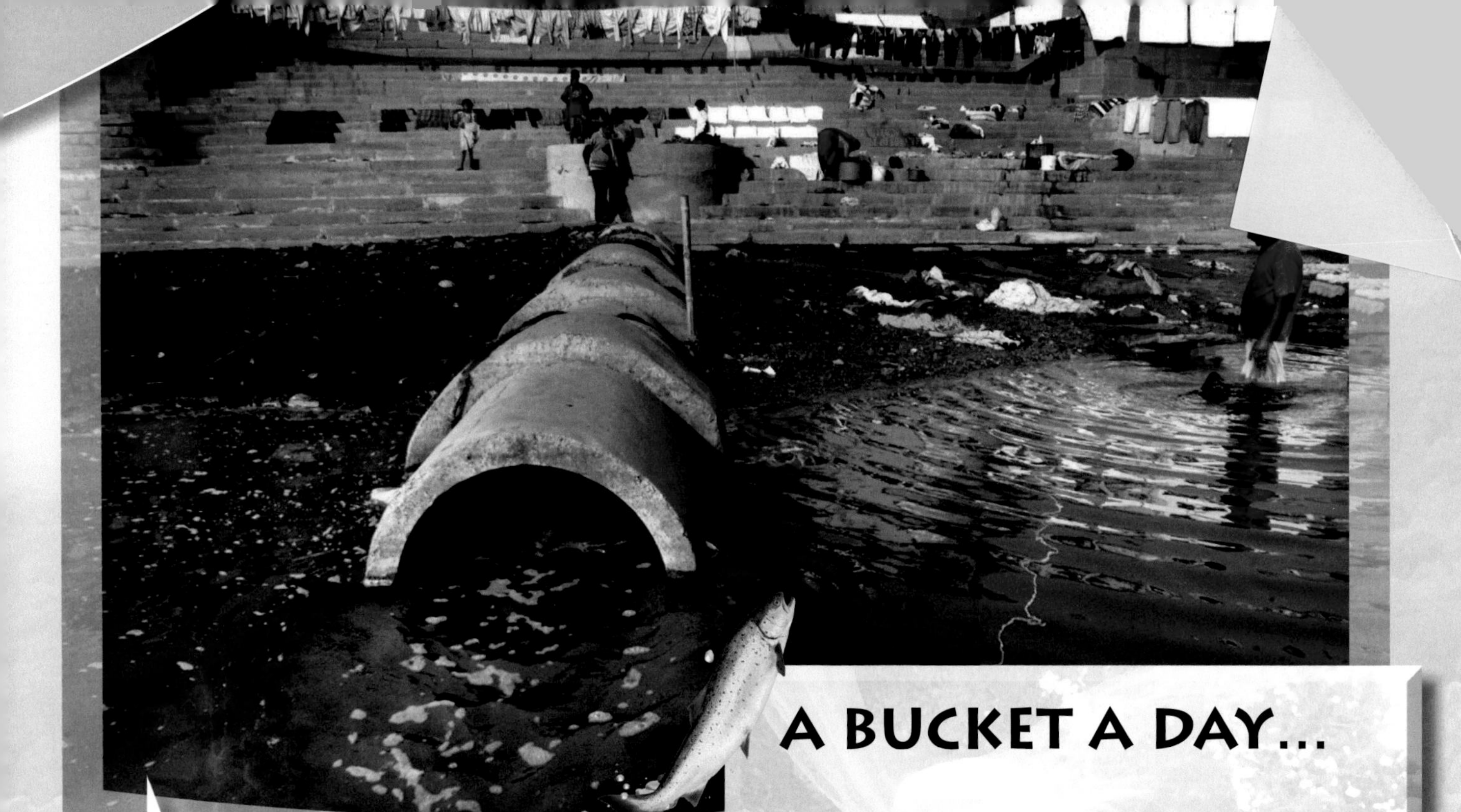

Raw sewage and industrial waste flow into the Ganges River in Varanasi, India. Hindus believe the Ganges is the holiest river, but it is now also one of the most polluted.

A BUCKET A DAY...

What do you do to get clean, fresh water? You probably just turn on the tap! Twelve-year-old Ahmed, who lives in Sudan, walks 10 km every day to a river to collect water for his family. Then he walks back home carrying the bucket of water. The bucket holds 10 litres of water and weighs 10kg. That's the same as carrying ten bags of sugar.

Along with rubbish thrown into rivers, these chemicals make the water unsafe to drink and may kill animals and plants that live in or near the rivers. Climate change is also causing some rivers to dry up, while other river water is trapped by dams to form reservoirs so people can generate electricity using the water.

It is important to protect rivers from pollution so that we, and future generations, can continue to use and enjoy them. Companies can clean up their waste products so chemicals do not end up in rivers. You, too, can help support rivers by using water wisely.

Explore a river!

Using a map

You can use a map to explore the landscape around rivers. Look at the map below. See how:

- the river meanders across the flood plain
- a factory is built near the river
- a canal joins the river near its mouth
- the river mouth widens into an estuary as the river meets the sea

Look at a map of your local area, and answer these questions:

1) What is the name of the river nearest to where you live?
2) Where is its source?
3) Does the river join up with any other rivers?
4) Can you name three settlements that are sited along the river?
5) Are there any bridges across the river?
6) Where does the river reach the sea?

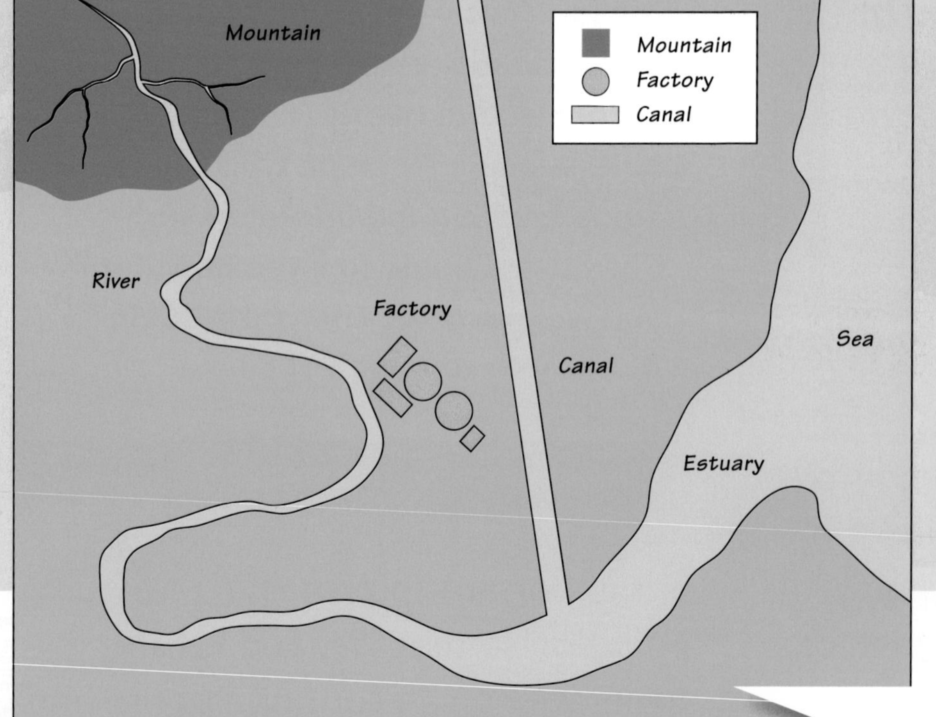

The map on this page charts the course of a river from its source high in the mountains to the sea.

Go to a local river

Go for a walk by your local river with your class or family. Take a look around and see how many different plants and animals you can spot.

Warning
Always tell an adult where you are going before you go for your river walk. Never go out alone and do not swim or wade in the river.

What kinds of river plants can you see? Can you spot any fish in the water? Can you see any water birds? You could compare the wildlife found by your local river to a river in a different part of the world.

People like to use rivers, too. Can you see anyone fishing or any boats on the water? What other ways is the river used for leisure?

Rivers are home to many different plants and animals, such as these ducks.

Cross-curricular links

Use this topic web to investigate rivers in other parts of your curriculum.

RIVERS

Citizenship
Make a poster to show how everyone can save water at home.

English & ICT
Use the Internet to investigate a flooding incident. Write a newspaper report to describe what happened and design it as a newspaper article.

Art
Draw a picture of a river in the style of a famous artist such as Claude Monet or Pablo Picasso.

History
Use the Internet or books from your library to find out about the ancient Egyptians and how they depended on the River Nile. Write a 'day in the life' account in the words of an Egyptian farmer or fisherman.

Design & Technology
Draw a map of a river near to where you live. Mark on the source, any bridges, farms, villages and towns on your map. Draw pictures or take photographs of things you can find along the course of the river and stick them on your map.

Science
Explore the feeding relationships between the different plants and animals that live by rivers. Draw a food web to show how they are related.

Glossary

Condensation To change from a gas to a liquid.

Current The main flow of water in a river.

Dam A wall built across a river.

Delta The place where the river deposits its load as it enters the sea.

Deposition When a drops sand, pebbles and silt to form a sand or gravel beach.

Drought When little or no rain falls over a long time.

Erosion When a river wears away the land.

Estuary A place where the river's mouth widens and enters the sea.

Evaporation To change from a liquid to a gas.

Flash flood A serious flood that occurs quickly and without warning.

Flood plain Flat land next to a river that floods when the river bursts its banks.

Fossil fuel A fuel made from the remains of animals and plants that lived millions of years ago, e.g. Petroleum.

Global Warming A rise in the average air temperature of the Earth.

Habitat A place where animals and plants live.

Hydroelectricity Electricity produced from the energy of flowing water.

Irrigation When farmers water their fields to grow crops.

Load All of the material carried by a river.

Meander A wide S-shaped bend in a river.

Monsoon The rainy season which accompanies seasonal winds in India and south-east Asia.

Oxbow lake A curved lake that forms when a river cuts off the loop of a meander.

Plunge pool A deep pool at the bottom of a waterfall.

Pollution Dumping harmful and unsafe substances into the environment.

Precipitation The term for rain, snow, sleet and hail.

Reservoir A lake that forms when a dam is built across a river.

River cliff A steep bank on the outside of a meander, formed by erosion of the river bank.

Sediment Material such as sand and mud.

Silt is a very small material carried by a river.

Spring The point at which an underground river or stream emerges at the Earth's surface.

Tides The rise and fall of the sea or ocean.

Transportation When the river's load is carried along by its current.

Tributary A smaller river or stream that joins a larger river.

Turbine A machine for making electricity that can be driven by wind, water or steam.

Waterfall Water falling from a height. It forms when a river flows over hard rock, then over softer rock.

Index

Further information

Books

River (Your Local Area) by Ruth Thomson, Wayland, 2010

Rivers (Our Earth in Action) by Chris Oxlade, Franklin Watts, 2009

Rivers (Starting Geography) by Sally Hewitt, Franklin Watts, 2009

The World's Most Amazing Rivers by Anita Ganeri, Raintree, 2010

Websites

Find out about rivers and coastal habitats on the BBC website:

http://www.bbc.co.uk/schools/riversandcoasts/

The Enchanted Learning website has facts about rivers and the water cycle:

http://www.enchantedlearning.com/

Geographywise

Contents of titles in the series:

Coasts 978 0 7502 6265 1
What are coasts?
Shaping the shore
Bays and headlands
Cliffs, arches and caves
Beaches, dunes and deltas
Islands and coral reefs
Seaside weather
Wildlife on coasts
Using the coast
Living on coasts
Dangerous coasts
Taking care of coasts
Explore life at the seaside!
Cross-curricular links
Glossary
Index and Further information

Mountains 978 0 7502 6266 8
What are mountains?
Fold mountains
Block mountains and rift valleys
Volcanoes
Wearing away
Carved by ice
Mountain weather
Mountain wildlife
Living in the mountains
Working in the mountains
Mountain dangers
Taking care of mountains
Explore a mountain!
Cross-curricular links
Glossary
Index and further information

Deserts 978 0 7502 6267 5
What are deserts?
How do deserts form?
Rocky deserts
Sandy deserts
Ice deserts
Weather in deserts
Where is the water?
Desert animals and plants
Living in the desert
Using deserts
Dangerous deserts
Deserts: good or bad?
Exploring a desert!
Cross-curricular links
Glossary
Index and Further information

Rivers 978 0 7502 6264 4
What are rivers?
From mountain to sea
The water cycle
Shaping the land
On the flood plain
A river meets the sea
River wildlife
Living by rivers
Moving around
River power
Problems with rivers
Damaging rivers
Explore a river!
Cross-curricular links
Glossary
Index and further information

WAYLAND

3 8002 01874 9814